IMAGES
of America

REDONDO BEACH POLICE DEPARTMENT

Various badges used by the Redondo Beach Police Department since its beginning in 1892 are depicted here. (Photograph courtesy of the Harry Petersen collection.)

On the Cover: The Redondo Beach Police Department is shown in 1942. From left to right are (first row) Sgt. Ollie Cole and patrolmen Robert Mutch, Ted Wester, and Frank Sturtevant; (second row) Sgt. Jack Dill; Sgt. Edward McAlister; Assistant Chief A. L. Hopkins; Capt. Eli Dessery; Sgt. Olin Scrivens; patrolmen Curt Richardson and James DeMers; Chief Harry Petersen; special officer Harry W. Petersen; patrolmen Harvey Bolmer, Harry Dean, and Harry Smith; and Sgt. Benjamin Kerley. (Photograph courtesy of the Redondo Beach Police Department.)

IMAGES
of America

Redondo Beach Police Department

Michael L. Stark and
Capt. John Skipper, Ret.

ARCADIA
PUBLISHING

ISBN 978-0-7385-8164-4

Published by Arcadia Publishing
Charleston, South Carolina

Printed in the United States of America

Library of Congress Control Number: 2010928641

For all general information, please contact Arcadia Publishing:
Telephone 843-853-2070
Fax 843-853-0044
E-mail sales@arcadiapublishing.com
For customer service and orders:
Toll-Free 1-888-313-2665

Visit us on the Internet at www.arcadiapublishing.com

This book is dedicated to the men and women, sworn and non-sworn, of the Redondo Beach Police Department who have worked to protect the residents and to assist in the provision of a quality of life that benefits everyone who lives in or visits our city. The authors would like to specifically dedicate this to Amador Espinosa, a World War II veteran who has dedicated more than 55 years of service to the department. Amador has served as the administrative assistant to nine chiefs of police and continues to serve as of this date as a volunteer.

Contents

Foreword		6
Acknowledgments		8
Introduction		9
1.	The Early Years: 1892–1920	11
2.	The Roaring Twenties and Depression Era: 1921–1940	17
3.	The Boomers: 1941–1960	27
4.	Modernization Begins: 1961–1980	45
5.	The Technology Era: 1981–2000	69
6.	A New Millennium, Our Future Begins: 2001–Present	97
Chiefs of Police		127

Foreword

The city appointed its first peace officer in May 1892, and the men and women of our department have served the Redondo Beach community with distinction to our profession for more than 118 years. Our members have been, and continue to be, an integral part of our community; one does not succeed without the other. Redondo Beach is the ninth oldest city in Los Angeles County. Our department and our community have touched the lives of millions of people throughout Southern California in every decade and every generation. Redondo Beach has always been a destination as a beautiful place to live, work, and visit. We invite you to share our history in the photographs of this book.

We are a department with character. Behind every face is the story of an individual with the strengths and weaknesses shared by all. These are the faces of courage and heroism, honesty, integrity, ethics, honor, courage, respect, fairness, and compassion. These are the faces of advocates in the cause of justice, acting with resolve to achieve excellence in policing. These photographs, with stories of humor, boredom, terror, and tragedy behind them, are glimpses of our experiences as dispatchers, peace officers, clerks, jailers, and the many other essential members of our department. We have shared the best and the worst moments of people's lives, often contacting our customers as complete strangers and leaving as involved partners in the most intimate, personal, and important moments of their lives. We have shared moments of the deepest sorrow and the greatest happiness among each other and with people we might never meet again. Enjoy the book. Throughout our history, Redondo Beach is the little place where big things happen. We are the men and women of the Redondo Beach Police Department, in service to our community and pursuing the highest values of the law enforcement profession.

—W. Joseph Leonardi
Chief of Police, Redondo Beach, California
May 2010

Chief Joe Leonardi started his career with the Redondo Beach Police Department in October 1982. He worked many officer assignments, including patrol, DUI enforcement, motors, beach and gang enforcement details, and investigations. He managed the development of many of the department's computer technology projects, including Computer Aided Dispatch and Records Management Systems, acquiring patrol vehicle computers, expansion of radio and communications infrastructure, geographic information systems, document imaging, and interfaces to other state and local databases. "We stand on the shoulders of those who served before us, and work is easy when you are doing something that you love—law enforcement," Leonardi said.

Acknowledgments

The authors wish to acknowledge the men and women of the Redondo Beach Police Department who have assisted in the creation of this book by providing pictures, information regarding events, or the identification of people in the photographs. The authors also wish to acknowledge in particular three individuals without whose efforts the creation of this book would not have been possible: Capt. Jeff Hink was the liaison with the department command staff and facilitated interaction with the various work units while contributing many hours of involvement to finish our task; retired lieutenant Gary Wiley who, as the committee historian, was instrumental in identifying many of the events and people in this book; and officer Maureen Hyde, who provided technical and computer support by organizing, scanning, archiving, and photograph shopping the many photographs in this book. These three met with the authors as a committee every week for approximately six months in the creation of this work.

And finally, a special thank you to the Harry W. Petersen family, the Redondo Beach Historical Society, and the Redondo Beach Historical Commission for their major contributions in providing historical photographs and information. Unless otherwise credited, the photographs on these pages were from the files of the Redondo Beach Police Department.

INTRODUCTION

The city of Redondo Beach is located in the southwest portion of Los Angeles County, approximately 20 miles from downtown Los Angeles. Founded on April 29, 1892, Redondo Beach is the ninth oldest city in the county. Approximately 67,000 residents live within the 6.28-square-mile city boundaries.

Redondo Beach is a classic Southern California beach community known primarily for its rich surfing heritage and beach lifestyle, as well as one of the largest recreational piers in Southern California. Northrop Grumman, a defense contractor, is located in the northern portion of the city and is one of the biggest employers. There is also the large South Bay Galleria shopping center with upscale stores that attract shoppers from throughout the greater South Bay area. Some of the more famous (and infamous) former residents of Redondo Beach include actress Demi Moore, the Smothers brothers, and Lynette "Squeaky" Fromme (the former Manson family member who also tried to assassinate Pres. Gerald Ford).

The Redondo Beach Police Department traces its origins to May 9, 1892, just over a week after the city was incorporated. At that time, S. P. Rogers was appointed as the first city marshal. By the Roaring Twenties, the city had become a major coastal resort complete with gambling casinos and organized crime. As the city grew and became more sophisticated, so did the police department. Harry M. Petersen, who became one of the first motorcycle officers for the department in 1918 and was eventually promoted to chief of police, can be credited with expanding and professionalizing the department during this era.

The department continued expanding and changing as the city evolved. Today, with over 200 sworn, non-sworn, and volunteer personnel, the Redondo Beach Police Department enjoys a reputation as one of the most capable and creative police departments in Los Angeles County. As you will see within the pages of this book, the RBPD has consistently developed proactive and innovative programs that have been recognized on national and even international levels while maintaining first-rate local law enforcement services as part of their commitment "To Protect and Serve" the citizens of Redondo Beach.

We hope you enjoy these images of a great police agency.

One

The Early Years

1892–1920

This c. 1880 view is looking south across the 100 block of North Alameda Avenue, later named Pacific Avenue. The tent in the background is on Emerald Street and is the location where city hall was built. (Photograph courtesy of Redondo Beach Historical Commission.)

The casino is seen from the water in the 1890s. Gambling was prevalent and was one of the concerns of the newly incorporated city. Ordinances were passed, but backroom operations were ongoing. With the Depression of the late 1920s, gambling made a come back with an ordinance that allowed it along El Paseo Street between Emerald and Diamond Streets. By 1940, the gamblers had been driven out, but carnival games and bingo remained. World War II ended any operations that still existed. (Photograph courtesy of Redondo Beach Historical Commission.)

The Redondo Beach Police Department's ranks increased from three to five officers in 1914 to police the 3,300 residents of the city. They were also referred to as deputy marshals or constables during this period. In the above photograph are, from left to right, Redondo Beach city marshal Ely Mosier; officers George Gipe, John V. Henry, and S. W. Kiracofe; and motorcycle officer Johnie Alder. (Photograph courtesy of Redondo Beach Historical Commission.)

Motorcycle officer Harry M. Petersen sits atop his *c.* 1918 police motorcycle. Motorcycle patrol began in 1914 as a result of an automobile race in the city, which drew residents from Los Angeles and other South Bay cities to the community. Newspaper accounts reported that traffic congestion "jammed the downtown section from one end to the other."

Shortly after the beginning of the 19th century, bathing suit morality became an issue across the country. In this photograph, a number of female sun worshipers are being escorted from the beach by members of the RBPD due to the hemlines of their bathing suits being deemed too high. (Photograph courtesy of Redondo Beach Historical Commission.)

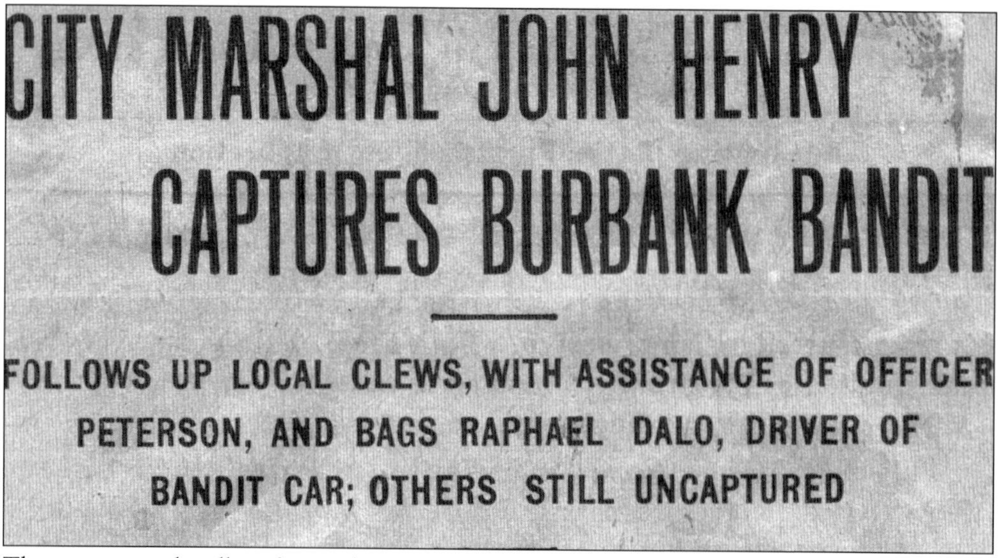
CITY MARSHAL JOHN HENRY CAPTURES BURBANK BANDIT

FOLLOWS UP LOCAL CLEWS, WITH ASSISTANCE OF OFFICER PETERSON, AND BAGS RAPHAEL DALO, DRIVER OF BANDIT CAR; OTHERS STILL UNCAPTURED

This newspaper headline from July 1920 tells the story of Chief John Henry capturing one of three bandits who robbed a Burbank bank and shot one customer. The article also mentions that officer Harry M. Petersen assisted with the arrest. Chief Henry inaugurated the department's first formal Identification and Records function. This unit organized reports, criminal records, and other important data, which Henry said were previously "just scraps of paper."

The city and the police department were growing. In the above photograph, city officials and police department personnel posed for a publicity shot taken around 1920. From left to right are (kneeling) Judge E. H. Miller, Chief of Police John V. Henry, and Mayor George Cate; (standing) officers Charles Beebe, Fred Reeves, Fred Gardener, George Carson, and Louie Stiewell and motorcycle officer Harry M. Petersen. Petersen went on to become chief of police, and his son Harry and grandson Rick later became members of the department. (Photograph courtesy of Redondo Beach Historical Commission.)

A 1920 photograph depicts motor officer Leslie Stewart and motor sergeant Harry Petersen.

In this undated photograph, a Redondo Beach motor officer sits on his department motorcycle outside city hall.

Redondo Beach officers are seen during monthly firearm qualifications at the range around 1920. In this photograph, officers are shooting down range in the direction of the current location of Beryl Street, just south of 190th Street. Dominguez Hill is to the rear.

The Redondo Beach Police Department is pictured here in 1920. From left to right are (first row) Sgt. Fred Reeves, Chief of Police John V. Henry, and officer Charles Beebe; (second row) motor officer Harry M. Petersen; Judge E. H. Miller; police matron Eva Kopp; officers Fred Gardner, Louis Stiewell, S. W. Kiracofe, and B. F. Booth; and motor officer Johnny Alder.

Two

The Roaring Twenties and Depression Era

1921–1940

The Redondo Beach Police Department is depicted in 1923–1924. From left to right are (first row) matron Eva Kopp, motor officer Harry Petersen, Sgt. Pete McCoy, Chief of Police John V. Henry, Sgt. Fred Reeves, and officer Johnny Alder; (second row) officers Charles Beebe, Fred Gardner, Ori Singer, B. F. Booth, and Roy Culver; motor officer Leslie Stewart; and officers L. C. Cobb and S. W. Kiracofe.

Redondo Beach Police Department is pictured above in the mid-1920s. From left to right are (first row) detective Johnnie Adler, motor sergeant Harry M. Petersen, Sgt. S. W. Kiracofe, Chief of Police John V. Henry, Sgt. Fred Reeves, officer Fred Gardner, and matron Eva Kopp; (second row) officers Charles Beebe, Louie Stiewell, B. F. Booth, and Roy Culver; motor officer Leslie Stewart; and officers L. C. Cobb, Pete McCoy, and Ori Singer.

These officers are working an extra detail on a motion picture set for Metro-Goldwyn-Mayer Studios in the 1920s. The scene they were filming was by the drawbridge in Wilmington. Pictured from left to right are Sgt C. Carpenter, LAPD; motor sergeant Harry Petersen and motor officer Leslie Stewart, RBPD; motor officer Severnes, L.A. County; MGM movie director (seated in the car); motor officer Calbreth, L.A. County; motor officer Steele, L.A. County; and motor officer Johnny Foot, Hermosa Beach PD.

Redondo Beach police sergeant Charles Beebe acts as desk sergeant in this early photograph. The concept of one sergeant on each shift was instituted in the early 1920s so there would always be a ranking officer present. During this period, the only way to contact an officer patrolling the city was for the telephone operator or sergeant to press a button that activated an "electric gong," which sat atop city hall. The gong could be heard for approximately five blocks. Upon hearing the gong, the officer would call the operator or sergeant to be dispatched to his call.

This January 20, 1926, newspaper headline tells the story of Redondo Beach officers S. W. Kiracofe and Louie Stiewel, who were involved in the shooting of an El Segundo man after he attacked his family and then shot at the officers, narrowly missing them. The story goes on to indicate that the officers attempted to save this suspect even after he tried to kill them. (Photograph courtesy of the Redondo Beach Historical Commission.)

OFFICERS KIRACOFE AND STIEWEL SHOOT CRAZED MAN AFTER HE ATTACKS

El Segundo Man Resisted Arrest, Charge of Threats Against Family and Officers, It Is Reported

MAN DIES FROM TWO BULLET WOUNDS

Redondo Policemen Try to Save His Life After They Had Replied to His Hail of Rifle Bullets

The Redondo Beach Police Department fielded a baseball team. Pictured from left to right are (first row) motor officer Leslie Stewart, officer B. F. Booth, Chief John V. Henry, and officers Maynard Henry, Johnny Alder, and Fred Gardener; (second row) officers Roy Culver, L. C. Cobb, motor officer Harry Petersen, and officers Louie Stiewell, Pete McCoy, Ori Singer, and S. W. Kiracofe.

A community parade was photographed in the 1930s. The young man in the center wearing the white uniform is Harry W. Petersen, the son of Chief Harry M. Petersen. Harry W. Petersen would later become a Redondo Beach police officer, retiring at the rank of captain.

A hobo camp in El Nido Park was an unfortunate offshoot of tough times during the Great Depression. Pictured are Sgt. Harry Halla (far left) and Chief Harry Petersen (far right). This picture shows a portion of the living quarters.

In the 1930s, William and Dorothy Howard were arrested for burglary. The suspects are looking over the loot, valued at $1,000, recovered when police raided their 515 ½ Hermosa Avenue (now known as Harbor Drive) apartment. Pictured are guns, watches, jewelry, and stolen clothing behind the officers. Standing behind the Howards are, from left to right, the officers who made the arrest, sergeants Jack Smith, Harry Hall, and Harry Beerup and Chief Harry M. Petersen.

Chief Harry Petersen (left) and Chief Eddie Messenger of the Hermosa Beach Police Department are pictured here in police cars of the era.

Illegal alcohol stills were a law enforcement problem in Redondo Beach as they were in other jurisdictions during Prohibition. This display of equipment used in liquor production was found in a local raid. Pictured from left to right are Chief J. V. Henry, officer Louie Stiewell, motor officer Harry Petersen, detective Johnny Adler, and officer Fred Gardner.

Another photograph depicts equipment found at a local moonshine still. Pictured from left to right are Justice of the Peace Browning, motor officer Harry Petersen, officer Fred Reeves, Chief John V. Henry, detective Harry "Silk Hat" Lowe, and officer Fred Gardner.

The 1930 Redondo Beach Police Department poses for a picture. From left to right are (seated) motorcycle sergeant H. Beerup, Sgt. H. Halla, Chief of Police Harry M. Petersen, A. L. Hopkins, and Jack Smith; (standing) motorcycle officer T. Chittenden and officers O. L. Scrivens, A. Clutter, E. R. Carter, J. L. Frederick, O. Cole, and I. D. Kersey.

Redondo Beach police officer Ernest Carter is depicted here around 1930.

The Redondo Beach Police Department in 1938 included, from left to right (first row), officer J. F. Dittemore, Sgt. A. L. Williams, and officer C. S. Thomas; (second row) officer L. A. Eannor, Capt. A. L. Hopkins, Chief H. M. Petersen, Capt. E. J. Dessery, and officer O. Alford; (third row) sergeants O. L. Scrivens, W. J. Balaam, O. G. Cole, and matron Pearl Krids; (fourth row) officers B. A. Kerley, F. Stuartevant, J. W. Dill, E. Shortridge, and E. Nealister.

Chief Harry M. Petersen (left), officer O. L. Scrivens (center), and motorcycle sergeant Virgil Hays are seen with the results of a still operation raid at a residence in the 700 block of the Esplanade. Officers found 50 gallons of industrial alcohol, blending compounds, and paraphernalia for making illegal whiskey.

During the 1930s, a variety of gambling barges were anchored off the coast of Long Beach and in Santa Monica Bay. The SS *Rex*, a well-known gambling barge anchored off Redondo Beach, was owned by mobster Tony Cornero. He bought the barge, totally remodeled it, and opened it off Redondo on May 5, 1938. It could hold 2,000 passengers and had a crew of 325. A water taxi provided transport from Redondo Beach for a fee of 25¢, and the gambling barge reportedly netted $300,000 per month. L.A. district attorney Buron Fitts and Sheriff Eugene Biscailuz worked to shut down the gambling barges. In 1939, state attorney general Earl Warren led the fight in the courts and won a ruling outlawing the gambling barges. By late 1939, the barges had been shut down. The U.S. Navy later used the Rex as a cargo barge during World War II; it was captured by a German submarine and sunk off the coast of Africa.

OFFICIAL BULLL IN
Civil Service Examination
City of Redondo Beach
Los Angeles County Civil Service Commission

Vol. 1 — March 30, 1939 — No. 1

The Civil Service Commission of the County of Los Angeles will hold the examination indicated below for the City of Redondo Beach.

Applications may be secured, acknowledged, and filed at the office of the Personnel Clerk, Office of the Mayor, City Hall, Redondo Beach, California.

Applicants must, at the date of filing applications, be CITIZENS of the UNITED STATES and bona fide RESIDENTS of the CITY OF REDONDO BEACH, CALIFORNIA, for AT LEAST ONE YEAR immediately preceding the date of filing applications, and MUST BE QUALIFIED ELECTORS OF THE CITY OF REDONDO BEACH, CALIFORNIA.

Successful applicants, before appointment to a permanent position, will be subject to a MEDICAL EXAMINATION.

Applicants in any examination failing to receive a final rating of 70% will be considered as having failed in such examination.

FILE YOUR APPLICATION AS EARLY AS POSSIBLE. In case of a tie in final rating, priority in filing determines priority on the list.

PATROLMAN

Includes Radio Car Patrol, Traffic Patrol, Traffic Direction, Investigating or Desk Duty, as assigned.

DEPARTMENT OF POLICE

Open Competitive Examination

LAST DAY FOR FILING APPLICATIONS—Friday, April 14, 1939, 5 p.m.

DATE OF EXAMINATION—Saturday, April 22, 1939, 8:30 a.m.

Examination Place—Report to Police Department.

SALARY: $125.00 per month during probationary six-month period. $137.50 per month thereafter.

DUTIES: Under the direction of the Chief of Police, to act as radio car patrolman, traffic patrolman, traffic director, investigator or desk officer, as assigned; to patrol assigned districts on foot or in a radio car; to give citations for traffic violations; to straighten out traffic congestions and check for violations of traffic laws and ordinances; to assist motorists having trouble on the streets and highways; to help clear streets and highways of obstructions and direct traffic on obstructed streets and highways; to do undercover work and investigate criminal cases; to make full and complete check on any information regarding complaints and cases; to check for prior records of suspects; to interview victims of crimes, accidents, etc., prisoners and suspects and obtain signed statements when possible, or when deemed advisable; to prepare cases for proper presentation in court; to apprehend law breakers, transport prisoners and serve legal process; to keep a daily log entering all complaints; to make out warrants and file reports; to act as Court Bailiff and Jailer; and to perform such other related duties as may be required.

REQUIREMENTS: Only applicants who fully meet the following requirements are desired for this service:

AGE: At least 21 years and not over 35 years at date of examination (23 to 30 years preferred). **SEX:** Male.

EDUCATION: Full high-school course or equivalent education. One year of continuous successful experience as a paid police officer, special agent or criminal investigator may be substituted for each year of high school lacking.

GENERAL QUALIFICATIONS: Applicants must be strong, active men who are physically sound; have well-balanced personalities and good health; be of good appearance, character and habits; have a knowledge of the functions and obligations of the Police Department; be familiar with the California State laws relating to law enforcement, civil, criminal and court procedure, crime classification, etc.; have a knowledge of the use and care of rifles, guns and revolvers; be able to operate an automobile skillfully; have the ability to exercise clear, quick thinking in emergencies; be able to make investigation of complaints and criminal cases in an efficient manner; have the ability to keep accurate records and to make clear and comprehensive written reports; be tactful, diplomatic and firm in dealing with others; have the personality and ability to meet the public courteously and intelligently; be responsible, reliable and resourceful; have integrity, initiative and good judgment; and be able to cooperate and work with other employees of the department in a harmonious manner.

Applicants must be qualified electors of the City of Redondo Beach.

Successful applicants in this examination will be fingerprinted before appointment.

PHYSICAL REQUIREMENTS: Applicants' physical measurements must conform with requirements of the following tabulation:

Height	Weight Minimum	Weight Maximum	Height	Weight Minimum	Weight Maximum	Height	Weight Minimum	Weight Maximum
5 ft. 9 in.	145 lbs.	179 lbs.	6 ft. 0 in.	160 lbs.	197 lbs.	6 ft. 3 in.	175 lbs.	215 lbs.
5 ft. 10 in.	150 lbs.	185 lbs.	6 ft. 1 in.	165 lbs.	203 lbs.	6 ft. 4 in.	180 lbs.	221 lbs.
5 ft. 11 in.	155 lbs.	191 lbs.	6 ft. 2 in.	170 lbs.	209 lbs.	6 ft. 5 in.	185 lbs.	227 lbs.

Applicants whose height, WITHOUT SHOES, falls between any of the above-stated measurements should meet the requirements of the lower as to weight. Applicants who do not come within the prescribed measurements should not apply for the examination as it can result only in rejection.

NOTES:
1. **Physical Tests:** All applicants will be tested as to physical strength and athletic ability during the day of the written examination.
2. **Medical Examination:** Before appointment to a permanent position applicants must pass a medical examination.
3. **Marksmanship:** Appointees must qualify in marksmanship at the official range during the probationary period of employment.
4. Applicants must submit with their applications their unmounted photographs taken within two years.

SCOPE OF EXAMINATION

		Relative Weights
1.	Written (or Oral) Examination	50%
2.	Physical Tests (separate and distinct from medical examination)	10%
3.	General Qualifications, Experience and Education, verified by interview and references	40%
	Total	100%

LOS ANGELES COUNTY CIVIL SERVICE COMMISSION,
CLIFFORD N. AMSDEN, Secretary and Chief Examiner.

(PLEASE POST THIS NOTICE IN A CONSPICUOUS PLACE)

This 1939 notice of a Civil Service Examination for a Redondo Beach police officer stated in the general qualifications that "applicants must be strong, active men who are physically sound," among other things. The monthly salary was $137.50. (Photograph courtesy of the Redondo Beach Historical Commission.)

This 1940 photograph, taken looking west across Benita Street, depicts the Redondo Beach Fire Department and the police department/city hall facilities on Emerald Street.

Three

The Boomers

1941–1960

Shown working the desk during Covered Wagon Days, an annual celebration of the frontier lifestyle, is Chief Harry M. Petersen.

Mounted for the Covered Wagon Days Parade are, from left to right, Sgt. Olin Scrivens, officer Jack Dill, Chief of Police Harry Petersen, Sgt. Ollie Cole, and officer Otis Alford.

Members of the department qualify at the city range around 1940.

The Redondo Beach Police Department is pictured here in 1942. From left to right are (kneeling) Sgt. Ollie Cole and officers Robert Mutch, Ted Wester, and Frank Sturtevant; (standing) sergeants Jack Dill and Edward McAlister; Assistant Chief A. L. Hopkins; Capt. Eli Dessery; Sgt. Olin Scrivens; officers Curt Richardson and James DeMers; Chief of Police Harry M. Petersen; special officer Harry W. Petersen; officers Harvey Bolmer, Harry Dean, and Harry Smith; and Sgt. Benjamin Kerley.

Police chief Harry M. Petersen is shown holding a sawed-off shotgun that he took from an ex-con after a gun battle at an auto court.

The Redondo Beach Police Department is depicted in the mid-1940s.

Pictured in this 1944 photograph are, from left to right, (seated) matron Pearl Kribbs, sergeants Olin Scrivens and Jack Dill, Capt. Eli Dessery, Chief of Police Harry M. Petersen, Assistant Chief A. L. Hopkins, and sergeants Ollie Cole, Benjamin Kerley, and Edward McAlister; (standing) patrolmen Frank Sturtevant, Curt Richardson, James DeMers, and Robert Mutch, special officer Harry W. Petersen, and patrolmen Harry Smith, Harvey Bolmer, Ted Wester, and Harry Dean.

In 1946, Howard Hughes's giant wooden airplane, the *Spruce Goose*, was manufactured in a variety of components and transported through Redondo Beach. In this picture, the tail structure is being transported on its side southbound on Elena Street (later named Pacific Coast Highway) at Vincent Street with the assistance of a Redondo Beach motor officer. In the background is the earlier structure for St. James Catholic Church.

On January 11, 1947, Chief Harry M. Petersen (in the suit) greets new recruits on their first day. From left to right are Harry W. Petersen (the chief's son), Earl Van Senus, John Bruno, and Deward E. Farmer.

In this 1950 photograph, detectives Ed Staal (left) and Jack Renke (center), accompanied by Lt. Lee Carron, examine the marijuana plants they confiscated from a home on Steinhart Avenue following the arrest of the occupants.

Officer Harry Peterson and the Redondo Beach Police Department's state-of-the-art communications center are pictured here around 1949.

Members of the police department attend their monthly range qualification at the police department range located on Beryl Street, below Dominguez Park.

At the close of World War II, this mounted posse was formed to assist local police departments in the search of open fields or rough terrain for evidence or victims of foul play. Members shown are, from left to right, color bearers Earl Smith, George Yates, and Jimmy Pasarell and Curt Richardson,

Pictured are officers Harry W. Petersen (left) and Jack Renke with a modern police car. Longtime Redondo Beach residents, both men attained the rank of captain during their careers.

Bill McClellan, Harold Gaston, Bob Stone, John Wentworth, Jack Corbin, Lloyd Anabelle, John Torres, Warren Green, Erno Kineman, Bob June, Grace Yates, Peggy Torres, Gertrude Richardson, Helen Wininger, Ola Wentworth, Betty Gaston, and Jane Green.

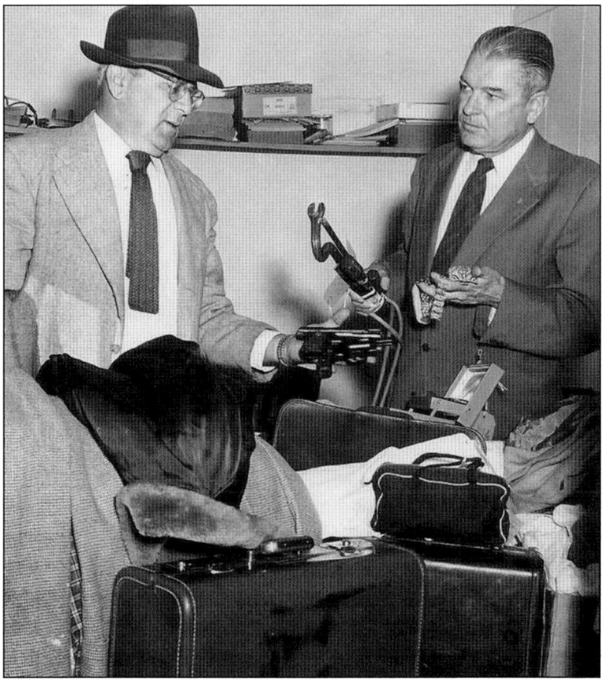

Lt. Bob Stone (left) and Chief Lowell Hopkins look over evidence in the property room around 1954.

City hall facilities were located on the top floor of the building in 1955, while the library was on the second floor and the police department was on the first floor and in the basement.

RBPD motor officer Henry "Flip" Chemnitzer is pictured here around 1955 on his police motorcycle behind city hall and the police station.

The first RBPD beach patrol vehicle is seen here. This photograph was taken on the Strand, west of the power plant. This area later became a portion of Port Royal Marina, which is now on Harbor Drive.

A 1955 RBPD unit is parked outside the police department on Emerald Street.

This 1955 department photograph was taken on the Redondo Union High School girls' softball

One of the community services that the police department provided was instruction on safe bicycle riding and the licensing of bicycles. In this 1957 photograph, officers can be seen assisting at the annual bicycle rodeo.

field, where the current police station now stands.

The RBPD Police Wives Pistol Team competition is seen above. Shooting are, from left to right, Frances Petersen, wife of Harry W. Petersen; Pauline Mutch, wife of Bob Mutch; unidentified; and Janie Renke, wife of Jack Renke.

This 1957 photograph depicts members of the RBPD. At that time, the department consisted of 44 sworn and 4 civilian employees. By the beginning of the 21st century, the department's workforce had grown to over 200 sworn, civilian, and volunteer members and was much more diverse and representative of the community.

Two new 1958 RBPD Ford police units are seen down by the waterfront. The area behind the cars is the future site of King Harbor.

A 1950s Harley Davidson tricycle was used for parking and traffic enforcement. This vehicle was used by patrol officers on an as-needed basis to augment the motor units.

Officer Ken Johnson speaks with officer Cosmo "Sparky" Sivolella behind the police station on Benita Street before going on patrol.

The police station, seen here around 1957 at Diamond Street and Pacific Coast Highway, was built at a cost of $266,000.

This photograph was taken during the formal opening of the new police station on December 19, 1959. Pictured are, from left to right, Burton W. Chace, Los Angeles County supervisor; policewoman Gladys Dalby; and clerk matrons Rose Reyes, Edith Hooper, Dorothy Dean, Dorothy Cheney, and Lillian Lord.

This photograph depicts the formal opening ceremony and flag raising at the new police station in 1959.

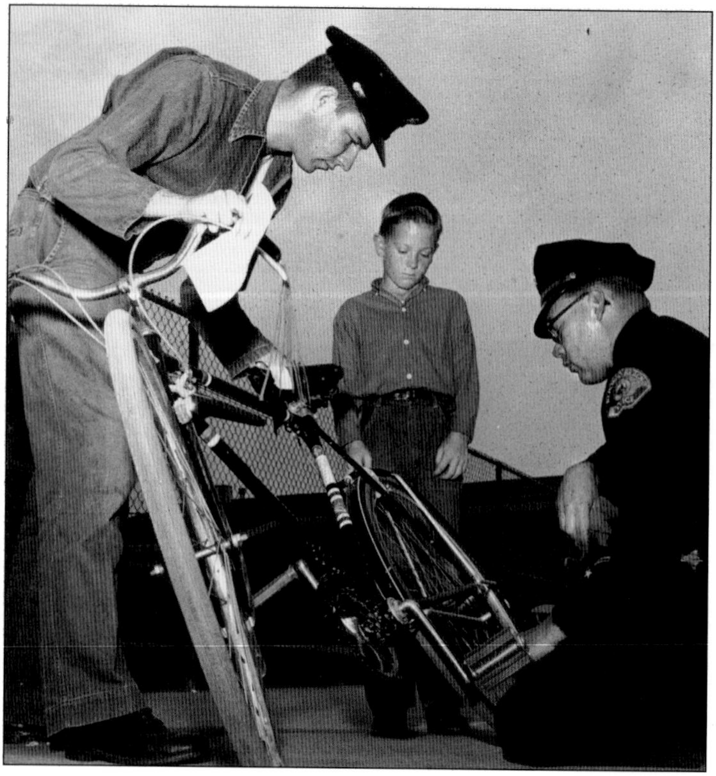

Officer Harry W. Petersen conducts a bike inspection at one of the local schools.

A 1950s photograph shows RBPD officer Robert Mutch and his wife, Pauline. Assistant Chief Mutch was instrumental in establishing the South Bay Mutch Fund, which provided immediate monetary relief to the family members of any officer who died while employed by a South Bay police agency.

Four

Modernization Begins 1961–1980

Russell Peltz began his career with RBPD in 1956. He became the department range master in 1959, a post he held until his retirement in 1984. This iconic photograph was taken in 1960 by a *Daily Breeze* photographer in Peltz's backyard on Harriman Lane.

Officer Bill Ehlers performs crossing-guard duties at Pacific Coast Highway and Emerald Street. In 1964, the city hired eight non-sworn crossing guards, establishing the program that is still in existence.

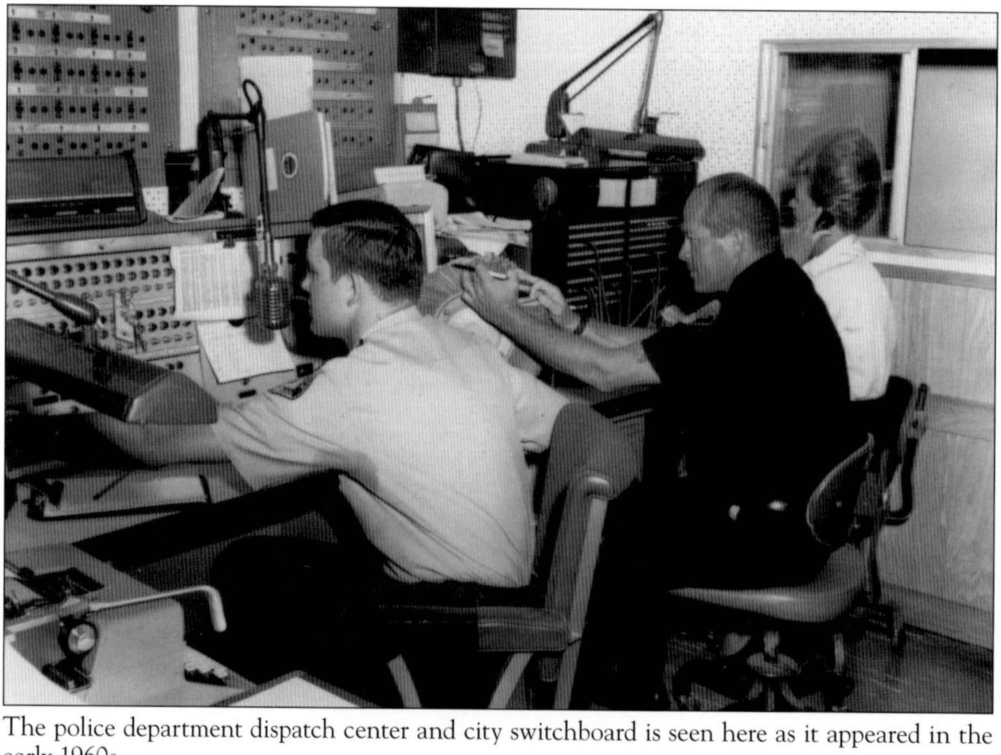

The police department dispatch center and city switchboard is seen here as it appeared in the early 1960s.

Firearms training is depicted in the early 1960s. Pictured are, from front to back, Eugene Cavenaugh, Cosmo Sivolella, Roy Thomas, Curt Richardson, and Florian Dirmann.

Officers Cosmo Sivolella (left) and Howard Lorenz are shown in front of the new station around 1961.

In the early 1960s, the police department was responsible for patrolling the harbor. Pictured here is officer Pat McGowen in the first Harbor Patrol boat.

The RBPD Pistol Team is seen in 1961. From left to right are officers Jerry Reese, Jim Porter, Russ Peltz, Roger Boston, and Bill Rico. While a member of this team, officer Peltz won the Practical Pistol Course overall trophy at a statewide law enforcement shooting competition held in Stockton.

On February 16, 1962, Redondo Beach police officers and matron clerks, led by Assistant Chief Robert Mutch (left) and Chief Curt Richardson, march to the funeral services of Manhattan Beach police motor officer Richard "Timothy" Giles, who died in an on-duty traffic accident.

In this photograph from 1962, officer Bob Pierce is seen firing a "warning" shot at an orca. Several of these whales had wandered too close to the beach and were scaring the public. Officers took care not to actually shoot the whales.

Officers Don Ollerton (left) and Lloyd Robertson work the Harbor Patrol.

On April 20, 1968, one of the worst accidents in the history of Redondo Beach occurred in the 900 block of El Camino Real. Four people were killed and 11 injured in a four-car, chain-reaction accident caused by street racing. The number of victims exceeded the capacity of a single emergency room, requiring emergency responders to call on four different South Bay hospitals to treat the victims. In the background is the future site of Alta Vista Park.

Sgt. Bob Pierce gives a briefing to officers Jerry Reese (left) and Don Adams (center).

Police cadet Bill Huddleston searches for a file in 1968. Prior to the advent of computerized record keeping, this large Rolodex file was considered state of the art and contained information dating back to the 1920s.

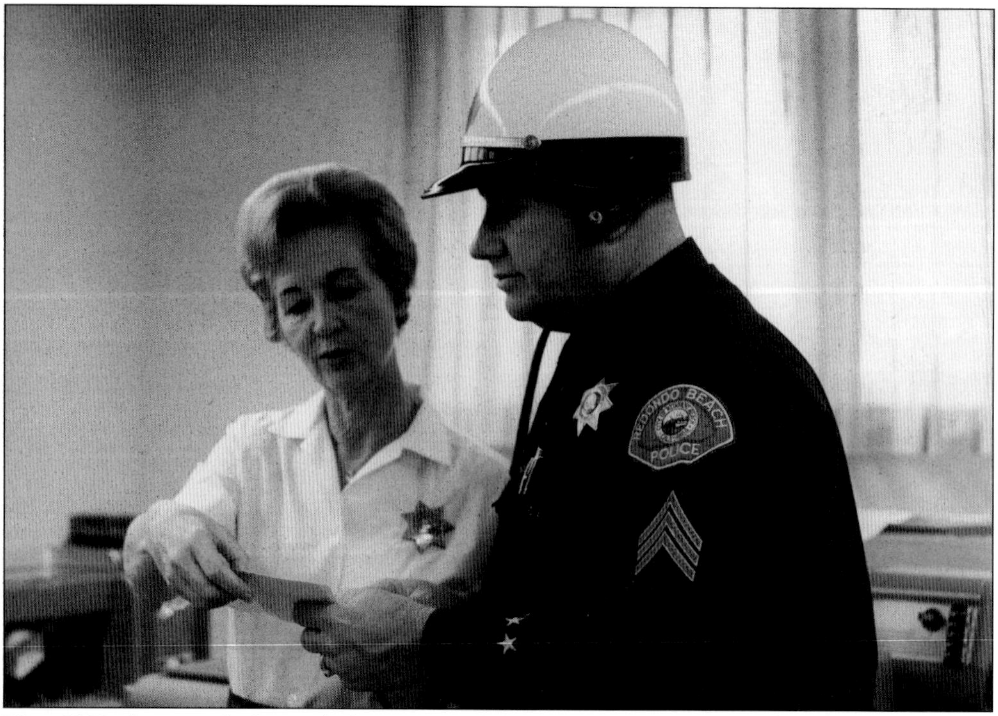

This 1968 photograph shows clerk matron Edith Hopper assisting Sgt. Earl Van Senus in the Records Bureau.

Officer Harry Petersen books a prisoner in the jail, assisted by Sonny Yanes, the department's first cadet. Yanes later returned to the department as a reserve officer.

In 1968, the Los Angeles Police Department formed Los Angeles County's first Special Weapons and Tactics (SWAT) Team. Shortly thereafter, sergeants Russ Peltz and Jerry Reese convinced Chief Lou Sunyich to establish an RBPD SWAT team. Shown here training at Camp Pendleton are, from left to right, original Redondo SWAT members officer Mike Minard, Sgt. Russ Peltz, and officers Doug Shore, Jim Rawson, and Bob Crigler.

After a 33-year career with the Los Angeles County Sheriff's Department (LASD) and a 10-year career with the Orange County District Attorney's office, Don Neureither joined the RBPD as a reserve officer in 2001, where he continues to serve well into his 70s. In this photograph from 1969, LASD sergeant Neureither (far left) is shown assisting in the arrest of Charles Manson.

Lt. Joe Wysocki sits at his desk in 1969. Wysocki was raised in an orphanage in New York and came to California as a young serviceman during World War II. While visiting Redondo Beach, he looked in the phonebook and found a Wysocki family in the city. They were not related, but the family invited him to Thanksgiving dinner anyway. Joe ended up marrying their daughter, Jerry, and settling down in Redondo, where they raised three children. Lieutenant Wysocki passed away in 1976 after more than 25 years with RBPD.

Pictured at their graduation from the Sheriff's Academy with Capt. Harry Petersen (center) are (in uniform) officers Ken Kauffman (left) and Jim Bell.

This station wagon was used to transport prisoners to court.

Officer Dave Miller and clerk matron Patti Natzman provide an up-close look at a police car for a group of children in the early 1970s.

Sgt. Russ Peltz supervises firearms training at the range *c.* 1970.

Officer Russ St. John poses for a publicity shot in front of the station with Redondo Union High School students and councilman Rod Neilson around 1969.

On June 13, 1971, Louis Belair sawed his way through steel bars and became the first person to escape from the RBPD jail. Belair fled through two unsecured steel doors and then vaulted the records counter. Belair was captured in December. (Photograph courtesy of *Daily Breeze*.)

ESCAPE FROM REDONDO

A 19-year-old arrested for armed robbery became the only person to break out of the city's jail

By Denise Nix
DAILY BREEZE

It took a slightly built robbery suspect with a lot of dedication to literally saw his way to becoming the first — and only — Redondo Beach jail escapee.

Louis John Belair was 19 years old in June 1971 when he was arrested for two armed robberies in Manhattan Beach.

An off-duty Redondo Beach police detective spotted Belair and his alleged accomplice, his brother Robert Ovilla Belair, 20, as he was driving on Inglewood Avenue near Carnegie Lane.

The Belair brothers were in a truck and the detective recognized one of them as being wanted for questioning in connection with the armed robberies of a sporting goods store and a market.

South Bay Yesterday

The detective called for assistance when the truck stopped at a residence, but the brothers left again before back-up units arrived. However, they soon noticed the barrage of patrol cars headed their way, stopped the truck and fled on foot.

Belair was caught, but his brother escaped immediate capture.

Three days later, Belair once again became a wanted man.

Early on a Sunday morning, his 16-year-old girlfriend visited him at the jail. They were speaking through a glass partition in the visiting room when, suddenly, Belair swung at the window, knocking the bottom loose and creating an opening at the base.

He told attendants he was angry at his girlfriend, who fled the station.

About seven hours later, as the 20 or so inmates of the then 11-year-old jail were being served dinner, a records clerk screamed as someone brushed past her, vaulted the counter into the lobby and ran out the front door.

Apparently, during the ruckus with his girlfriend, she slipped him a 5-inch-long piece of a hacksaw blade. Belair used it to cut an approximate 1-by-1-foot opening in the three-quarter-inch-thick steel bars of his cell door.

Then, the 5-foot, 6-inch, 145-pound Belair slithered out, tossed the sawed-off section into the drunk tank, opened two unlocked security doors and escaped. The hacksaw fragment was later found in a toilet paper roll in his cell.

His girlfriend was arrested when her parents brought her to the police station the next day, but Belair remained at large for five months until he inexplicably turned himself in to his parole officer.

Belair was booked on suspicion of robbery, destroying a jail, escape, assault wit a deadly weapon and violation of juvenile parole. In December 1971, he pleade guilty to two robbery charges and was sen tenced to five years in state prison in Apri 1972.

His older brother was arrested in October 1971 for driving a stolen car but hang himself in the Huntington Beach jail.

FILE PH

Diminutive prisoner Louis John Belair cut this 1-by-1-foot opening in his cell with a 5-inch fragment a hacksaw blade and slid out in 1971 to become the first, and only, Redondo Beach jail escapee

The dispatch center is seen in 1973. Pictured are Tracy Phee Stark (left) and Linda Hibbard. The dispatch center is responsible for handling all the calls for both police and fire departments.

Chief Lou Sunyich poses with a large seizure of marijuana and other drugs in 1972.

Patrolling the Redondo Beach Pier in 1972 are, from left to right, (front) officer Gary Wiley, Sgt. Joe Norris, and officer Doug Ritchie. Further back in the crowd are officers Ken Kauffman (left) and Mike Minard.

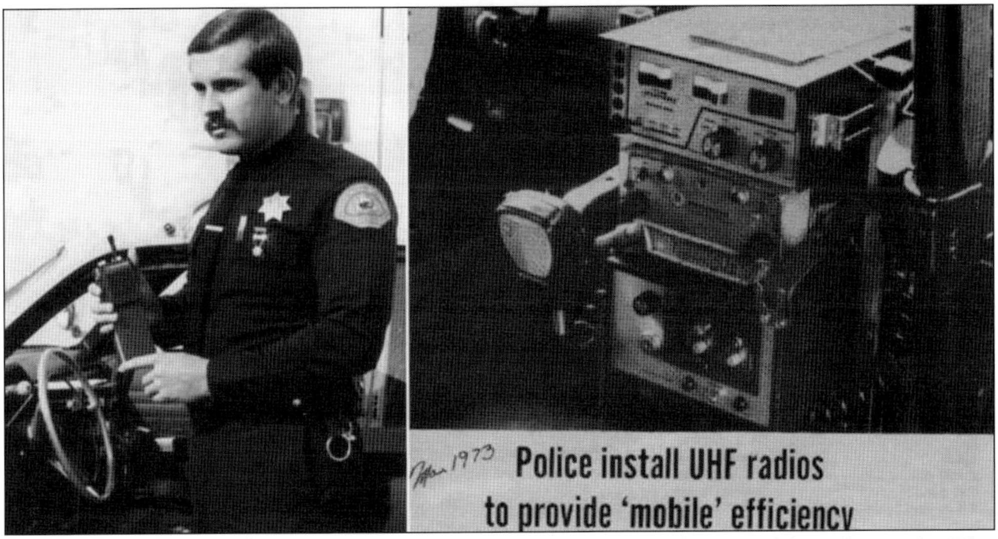

Officer John Welch is holding the new department radio in the portable radio mode. The accompanying newspaper article shows the configuration of the new police radio that was placed in each unit. These radios were unique, as they could be used as either the car radio or carried as a portable radio by pushing the release button next to the radio and removing it from the base.

Officer Mike Minard (with arm extended) inspects the RBPD Police Explorers in the early 1970s. Dave Atwater (far right) went on to become an RBPD officer and retired in 2007 after a 30-year career.

Pier patrol has been a unique and sought after "beat" for Redondo officers for decades. In this 1975 photograph, officer Roy Newton (left) talks to a citizen on the Redondo Beach Pier while officer Dave Miller waits in the Jeep, which was utilized for pier and beach patrol.

In 1975, RBPD hired its first two female police officers to be assigned general patrol duties: Patti Natzman and Dennis Roth. Shown here is officer Natzman at the range receiving training on the Remington 870 shotgun. Also pictured are, from left to right, officers Don Baird (partially concealed) and Sam Pitts and range master sergeant Russ Peltz.

Reserve officers Mike Stark (left) and Steve Murdoch perform a "vacation check" on a home in 1976. These checks were a service the department provided to offer residents peace of mind when they were out of town and away from their homes. (Photograph courtesy of the *Daily Breeze*.)

Officers are shown at a briefing in 1976. From left to right are (first row) officers Randy Martin and Tom Freeman; (second row) officers John Crawford, Ray Griffin, and Chris DeLoof.

Officer Gary Bounds, dressed for foul weather, gives his opinion in the Investigations Bureau during the 1970s.

The Chaplain Corps was created in 1974 by Chief Frank Meehan, who appointed Harold Hawkins as the first chaplain. The corps has been in existence since then, ministering to the needs of department and community members. From left to right are agent Avery Richey, chaplain Lee Huddleston, Lt. Ed Staal, and chaplains Leon Kahane and Liam Kidney.

The RBPD Canine Program, the second such program in the South Bay, was implemented in 1978 by Chief Frank Meehan and remains a mainstay of the department. Over the years, officers and their canine partners have been responsible for the arrest of hundreds of suspects and the seizure of thousands of pounds of narcotics and millions of dollars in U.S. currency used in narcotics transactions. Pictured are Redondo's first K-9 handler, agent Ken Kauffman, and his partner, Oscar, around 1978.

Chief Frank Meehan congratulates officer Steve Murdoch (in uniform) upon his graduation from the Riverside County Sheriff's Academy on March 2, 1978. Officer Murdoch started his career at RBPD as reserve officer. He retired in 2004 at the rank of captain, having also served as interim chief of police for a year.

Officer Rick Petersen graduates from the Riverside County Sheriff's Academy on March 2, 1978, keeping alive a tradition of Petersens in the RBPD—a tradition begun in 1918 when Rick's grandfather, Chief Harry M. Petersen, was hired as an officer. Harry W. Petersen, Rick's dad, served with the department from 1947 until 1976, retiring as a captain. Prior to becoming an officer, Rick worked as a police cadet and dispatcher. Rick retired in 2007 as a sergeant and continues to serve as a reserve officer. The Petersen family has been involved in the RBPD for more than 92 years.

The 1979 Redondo Beach Police Department softball team is seen here. The team has represented the department in various police softball tournaments and the Police Summer Games over the years.

Agent Jim Bell discusses police tactics with Oscar in 1978 while Oscar's handler, agent Ken Kauffman, observes.

Officer Phil Garcia (far right) poses with graduates of the RBPD Explorer program in 1979. Also pictured is Rody Contreras (second row, second from left), who is now a sergeant with the department. The RBPD Explorer program, which operated under the guidelines of the Boy Scouts of America, was designed to expose young people to potential careers in law enforcement.

Swing shift gets ready to go into the field in 1978. From left to right are officers Chris DeLoof and Jeff Meyers and agents Jim Rawson and Dave Pruitt with Pruitt's K-9 partner, Kaiser.

Agent Rich Sigler, while a member of the South Bay Burglary Team, poses with recovered firearms purchased in a successful undercover operation in the late 1970s.

On February 22, 1980, a suspect walked into the Bank of America at South Bay Center (now the South Bay Galleria) and shot and killed his girlfriend. The suspect then taped a shotgun to the neck of a hostage, surrounded himself with additional hostages, and exited the bank. SWAT members Sgt. Russell Peltz and agent Jim Rawson each fired fatal rounds at the suspect. Shown here, seconds after firing, is Sergeant Peltz behind the car. The suspect is on the ground in the center.

During SWAT training at Camp Pendleton in 1980, agent Ray Griffin was attempting a head-first, or "Australian," rappelling technique for the first time. In the excitement of the moment, agent Griffin simply dove off the rappel tower without holding onto the rope! His fall was stopped by his safetyman, agent Jim Rawson, just before Griffin hit the ground.

This photograph shows a K-9 training exercise at the Redondo Beach Pier parking structure in the early 1980s. From left to right, officer Randy Martin (in plain clothes) plays the role of the "bad guy" as reserve officer Bill Mona, officer Ken Greenleaf, and K-9 officer Boris take him into custody.

In this photograph, agent Ken Kauffman and his K-9 partner Oscar patrol the pier.

Five

The Technical Era 1981–2000

SWAT training took place at Camp Pendleton in 1980. Pictured from left to right are (kneeling) agent Steve Yoshida, officer Phil Garcia, and sergeants Russ Peltz and Jerry Reese; (standing) officer Bruce Rosin, agents Steve Stone and Ray Griffin, officers John Skipper and Chris DeLoof, and agents Rich Sigler and Jim Rawson.

This photograph taken in the early 1980s depicts various special assignments offered by RBPD. From left to right are motor officer Gordon Golding, traffic investigator Paul Burch, detective agent Phil Juvet, and agent Mike Higashi with his K-9 partner Axel. The SWAT van is seen in the background.

Agent Rich Sigler rappels down a 14-story building at a SWAT convention in Las Vegas. The department's "Mr. SWAT," Sigler served on the team for 30 years. On October 3, 1986, Sigler was shot in the right hand while trying to apprehend a gunman in South Redondo. Exactly one year later, he was dragged several blocks by a motorist as he was attempting to issue a citation. During his long career, Sigler worked every assignment an officer at RBPD could work with the exception of the pier.

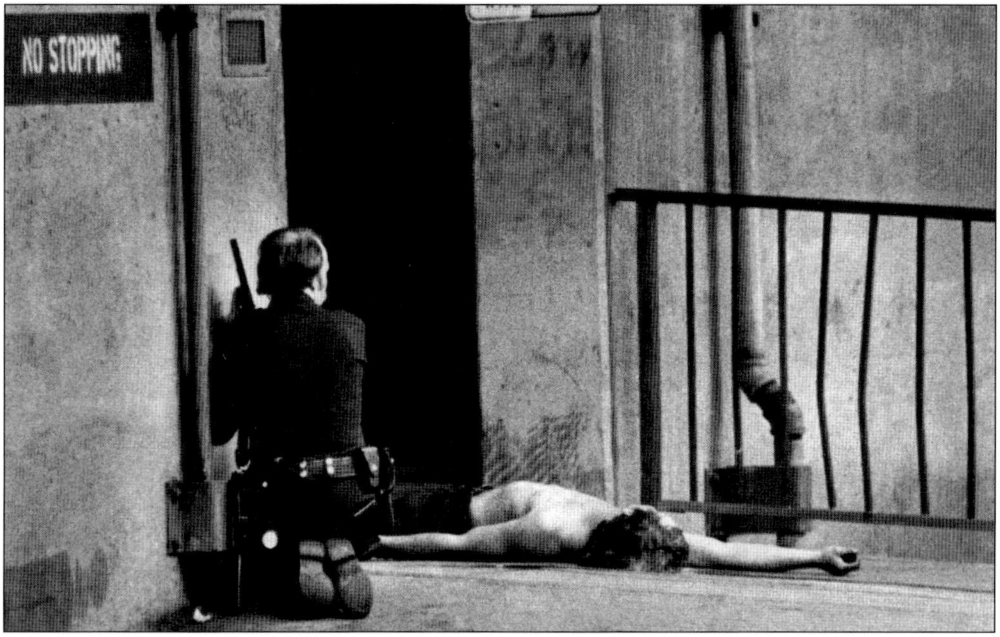

On January 12, 1981, Sgt. John Gordon and officer Don Martinez responded to a report of a robbery that occurred on the Redondo Beach Pier. As officer Martinez approached a suspicious vehicle in the parking structure, one of the occupants fired at him through the rear window, causing broken glass to fly into his face and eyes. Sergeant Gordon gave chase as the suspect fled. The suspect turned and engaged Gordon at point-blank range, wounding him in the side. Gordon returned fire, killing the suspect. Officer Mike Worford is seen here shortly after the shooting, during the search for additional suspects. Sergeant Gordon and officer Martinez were awarded the Medal of Valor for their actions. (Photograph courtesy of the *Daily Breeze*.)

Shown chatting at a retirement party for Lt. Ed Staal in 1982 are, from left to right, Amador Espinosa, the chief's administrative secretary, and Public Safety officers Lloyd Garner and Lucy Craig.

Pictured from left to right are agents Ray Griffin and Steve Yoshida and officer Dave Atwater at a graveyard briefing in the early 1980s.

A 1982 photograph depicts motor officer Leonard Knott with his son Matt. Matt, who followed in his father's footsteps, is currently an RBPD motor officer.

Agent Rich Sigler detains two individuals during the service of a search warrant in Lawndale in 1982. A Los Angeles County deputy sheriff backs him up.

In the mid-1970s, the Los Angeles County Sheriff's Department and several South Bay cities, including Redondo Beach, joined forces and formed the South Bay Burglary Team. This surveillance team followed and arrested known criminals committing "in progress" crimes such as burglary, robbery, and drug sales. Shown here after a narcotics search warrant in 1983 are, from left to right, Steve Yoshida, Tom Stevens (LASD), Craig Tranbarger (Manhattan Beach PD), Steve Murdoch (seated front), John Skipper, Mike Foster (LASD), and Bruce Rosin.

In 1983, the California Department of Justice began the Campaign Against Marijuana Planting (CAMP). This program organized law enforcement officers throughout the state in an effort to locate and eradicate marijuana-growing operations. Initially officers operated in remote Northern California counties, but over the years the program has expanded to include virtually every county in California. Agent Rich Sigler, seen here, represented Redondo Beach in the first year of the program. Since that time, Redondo Beach officers have participated in dozens of CAMP operations all over the state.

Officers participate in a charity donkey basketball game at Redondo Union High School between Redondo Beach officers and the Los Angeles Rams.

The grand opening of the Redondo Beach Pier police substation occurred in 1983. From left to right are Public Safety Officers (PSOs) Mike Diehr and Jan Carlson, agent Brian Buffer, Sgt. John Berry, and PSOs Silvia Villarreal and Rody Contreras.

The Reserve Corps was reinstated in 1973 with 10 new reserve officers. In this 1983 picture, the members of the Reserve Corps are being recognized by the Redondo Beach City Council for their dedication and volunteerism to the city. From left to right are (first row) reserve officers Ron Reading, Steve Shaylor, John Marshall, Greg Sirbu, Mary Rengel, John Meyers, Mike Clifton, Paul Decker, Harold Hawkins, and Mike Stark; (second row) reserve coordinating staff Sgt. Jeff Cameron, officers Mark Rodina and Don Martinez; and reserve officers Bill Mona, Warren Fields, Richard Salmon, Kent Perkins, Paul Ptak, and Paul Stewart.

In 1983, the Redondo Beach Police Officers' Association initiated a "job action" in response to stalled labor negotiations with the city. This action included picket lines manned by off-duty officers and pitching tents on the city hall lawn. Pictured here manning the picket line are, from left to right, Dennis Pappas, Jonathan Ott, an unidentified civilian supporter, John Wisser, Paul Burch, Fred Schumaker, Mike Worford, and Ron Krajcik. (Photograph courtesy of the *Daily Breeze*.)

This so-called "tent city" was pitched in front of Redondo Beach City Hall in 1983, protesting what was labeled "First in Service, Last in Pay." (Photograph courtesy of the *Daily Breeze*.)

RBPD motor officers are pictured around 1984. From left to right are officer Ron Krajcik, agent Jim Rawson, and officers Leonard Knott and Gordon Golding.

When the Olympic Games came to Los Angeles in 1984, the famous torch relay passed through Redondo Beach on its way to Los Angeles Memorial Coliseum for the opening ceremonies. Sgt. Russ Peltz was one of several Redondo residents to receive the honor of carrying the torch for one leg of the relay. He was accompanied by Sgt. Steve Murdoch, who can be seen to his right wearing a SWAT shirt.

The California Police Summer Games is an annual statewide event that encourages athletic competition among law enforcement officers. Many RBPD officers have competed in these games over the years and "brought home the gold" to Redondo Beach. Seen here is officer John Simmons earning his way to a gold medal in weight lifting. Watching off to the right is agent Ron Krajcik.

Lt. Ken Kauffman (in hat) inspects the RBPD Motor Unit in 1985. From left to right are Sgt. Randy Martin; officer Len Knott; agents Rich Sigler and Fred Schumaker; officers Mike Adye, John McIntosh, Craig Barnes, Todd Heywood, and Bob Sevilla; and traffic investigator Walt Sawall.

A patrol briefing is seen above in 1986. From left to right are (first row) agents John Wisser and Mike Higashi and Sgt. Paul Rossiter; (second row) officers Jim Toti, Fernando Mata, Jim Booth, Phil Garcia, and Cheri Mulligan; (third row) officer Phil Keenan.

In this 1986 photograph, Mayor Barbara Doerr is shown presenting awards to police cadets. Pictured are, from left to right, Steve Brey, Tony Campisi, Barbara Allen, Keith Turner, Bob Nishamura, and David Golf. Keith Turner is currently an RBPD officer. Cadets perform a variety of Support Services functions throughout the department.

In the mid-1980s, RBPD chief Frank Meehan created a Patrol Action Team (PAT). PAT worked in plain clothes and employed surveillance techniques to concentrate on crime problems such as burglaries and auto thefts throughout the city. Members of PAT in 1991 are, from left to right, (first row) agent Bill Wood and officer Phil Garcia; (second row) officer Jim Booth, Sgt. John Gordon, and officers Walt Sawall and Doug Peters.

In January 1986, a gunman barricaded himself in a residence in South Redondo Beach and began firing gunshots into the neighborhood. Redondo Beach SWAT officers could see that a woman was trapped on the second floor of the residence, unknown to the gunman. SWAT officers made a makeshift bridge to the residence by using a ladder and wooden planks, allowing them to cross over from an adjoining rooftop. While the Crisis Negotiations Team distracted the gunman, agent Bruce Rosin (on ladder) and Sgt. John Skipper crossed the ladder, placed a bulletproof vest on the endangered woman, and removed her to safety. Skipper and Rosin were each awarded the South Bay Medal of Valor for this incident. (Photograph courtesy of *Daily Breeze*.)

This 1980s photograph depicts the SWAT team participating in a CAMP operation in Humboldt County. From left to right are agent Bruce Rosin, officer Don Martinez, agent Mike Higashi, Sgt. John Gordon, agent John Wisser, and officers John Simmons, Phil Garcia, and Bob Sevilla.

In this 1988 photograph, Chief Roger Moulton, assisted by Lt. Steve Murdoch, inspects the Honor Guard. From front to back are officer Diane Atwater, agent Mike Higashi, officer Karen Brown, agent Mike Worford, and agent Dave Atwater.

The Drug Abuse Resistance Education (DARE) program was introduced in Redondo Beach in 1986. The program placed police officers in elementary and middle school classrooms to teach children the consequences of drug use and offer them more productive alternatives. DARE officers were encouraged to interact with the children, and many formed lasting relationships and served as positive role models to the children in their classes. Agent Rich Sigler can be seen here enjoying a game of basketball with some of his students.

SPORTS:

Agent Ray Griffin Wins Six Medals at National Police Olympics in Las Vegas

Agent Ray Griffin participated in the National Police Olympics this past September in Las Vegas, Nevada. Ray came home with 6 medals to his name, 2 golds and 4 silvers.

100 M	Silver
200 M	Silver
400 M	Gold
High Jump	Silver
400X100 M relay	Silver
400X1600 M relay	Gold

A proud Agent Ray Griffin displays his six medals.

Agent Ray Griffin, who came to RBPD from the Los Angeles Police Department in 1976, was a perennial medal winner in the California Police Summer Games. Ray is pictured here after winning six medals in 1988. During his career, agent Griffin earned over 60 medals.

THE Daily Breeze

A COPLEY LOS ANGELES NEWSPAPER

HOME EDITION
September 20, 1989 25¢
Torrance, California
95th year/Number 263
©1989 The Copley Press Inc.

WEDNESDAY

RB officer shot in gunbattle

Police kill suspect; 2nd victim found

By Stuart Dedic
STAFF WRITER

A veteran Redondo Beach police officer was shot and critically wounded moments before officers killed his assailant during a gunbattle Tuesday afternoon in a condominium where police found another man slain.

Officer Leonard M. Knott, 40, a 13-year veteran with the Redondo Beach force, was in "extremely critical" condition at County Harbor-UCLA Medical Center this morning after surgery, during which a bullet was removed from his neck, said police Lt. John Nelson.

Knott gave officers a "thumb's up" sign after surgery. This morning, he was passing notes with friends and other officers because his jaw has been wired shut and he cannot speak.

Neither the man who shot Knott nor the victim of the initial shooting was identified by police. Police said they suspect that the slain gunman killed the other man whose body was found in the doorway of the condominium just before the shots rang out.

Knott and two other officers were called to the condominium

cisca Avenue on a report shots being fired, said Redond Beach police Capt. Roger Bas

When the officers arrive about 1:35 p.m., they found th front doors locked and got pe mission from a sergeant knock them down. Inside, the noticed the body of a man the doorway who had been sh to death. Then an armed ma opened fire, striking Knott b low the left side of his botto lip, Bass said.

As the bleeding Knott lay

GUNBATTLE/A

Officer Leonard M. Knott wa wounded in the shootout.

edondo Beach Police SWAT team members enter the condo Tuesday. The man who shot Officer Leonard M. Knott was

On September 19, 1989, officers Leonard Knott, Mark Rodina, and Dave Taneman entered a condominium in the 300 block of North Francisca Avenue on a report of shots being fired. Inside they found an individual who had been shot to death. As they searched the condo, an armed man opened fire on them, striking Knott in the face with one round. Rodina and Taneman returned fire, killing the assailant. Officer Knott's wound ultimately forced him to retire. Officers Rodina and Taneman each received the South Bay Medal of Valor for their actions.

This is a 1980s photograph of the Records Bureau. From left to right are Lead Police Service Specialist (PSS) Nancy Krajcik, PSS Mechell Divinity, and officer Wayne Acosta working on a warrant detail. The Records Bureau is responsible for processing crime reports, booking information, and all computerized data transferred to and from other law enforcement agencies.

Officer Phil Keenan radios in information on possible gang members as officer Tom Krafick provides backup during a gang sweep in 1990. Redondo Beach has long been considered a leader in antigang enforcement programs among South Bay law enforcement agencies. This leadership role began in the 1980s as gang members throughout Los Angeles County began congregating in the pier and harbor area. Proactive enforcement and innovative programs such as a gang injunction have significantly reduced gang crime in the city since then. (Photograph courtesy of *Daily Breeze*.)

Officer Jim Booth is seen at a multi-jurisdictional traffic safety checkpoint around 1990.

A 1990s photograph depicts the Crime Prevention team. From left to right are Crime Prevention specialists Wilma Kochheim and Gina Cantabene, agent Ray Griffin, "McGruff" (also known as Larry Manley), and Crime Prevention specialist Stephanie Deason. Larry Manley, as the "McGruff" character, appeared on an episode of the television show *Webster* in 1986. (Photograph courtesy of *Daily Breeze*.)

Sgt. Don Baird and officer Phil Keenan (in jeans) handcuff a subject during a gang sweep in 1990. (Photograph courtesy of *Daily Breeze*.)

On December 9, 1992, RBPD officers, assisted by LAPD, take a bank robbery suspect into custody. After robbing the Redondo Beach bank, the suspect led officers on a pursuit to San Pedro, where he was captured. Pictured from left to right are an unidentified LAPD officer, officers Jeff Hink and Jim Booth, reserve officer Glen Thompson, an unidentified LAPD officer, and officer Steve Sabosky. (Photograph courtesy of *Daily Breeze*.)

The Command Staff participates in a meeting around 1991. From left to right are Chief Roger Moulton, lieutenants Larry Sprengel and Steve Murdoch, Capt. Roger Bass, Lt. Ken Kauffman, Capt. Ray Graham, Lt. Tom Doty, Sgt. John Skipper, and lieutenants Ken Keating and Jeff Cameron.

In January 1991, members of the RBPD Special Investigations Unit (SIU) were involved in a multi-kilogram undercover narcotics sting operation at Alpine Village in Carson when the four suspects produced guns and attempted to "rip off" the undercover officers. Backup officers returned fire, killing one suspect and wounding another. Two escaped but were eventually captured and sentenced to state prison. Shown here with Chief Moulton (second from left) receiving the South Bay Medal of Valor for their actions during that incident are, from left to right, officers Fernando Mata, Tom MacIsaac, Rick Mansfield, and Paul Hellinga.

The SWAT team conducts a training exercise in 1992. Pictured from left to right are (kneeling) agent John Wisser and officers Phil Garcia, Todd Heywood, and Bob Sevilla; (standing) agent Rich Sigler, officer Phil Keenan, Lt. Steve Murdoch, agent Wayne Windman, and officers Mike Adye, Jeff Hink, Tom Krafick, Jim Banach, and Terry Jones.

Graduating DARE officers are pictured with the Command Staff in 1991. Seen here from left to right are officer Tom Kantor, agents Ray Griffin and Wayne Windman, officer Cliff Dean, agent Paul Burch, Chief Roger Moulton, Lt. Ken Keating, and Capt. Roger Bass.

Chief's administrative secretary Amador Espinosa (holding plaque) receives recognition at the Dominguez Brands Awards banquet in 1993. With Amador are, from left to right, FBI Special Agent Marty Gallagher, Lt. Steve Murdoch, and Capt. Roger Bass.

Coming down the 190th Street hill during the 1993 Special Olympics torch run are, from left to right, Lt. Jeff Cameron, Chief Roger Moulton, officer Jeff Hink, and Lt. Ken Keating. The department participates in this annual event to help raise awareness for individuals with special needs.

Redondo Beach was the first South Bay city to implement the Citizens Academy Program, which allows participants to get a close look at how police work is conducted. This is the first graduating class on May 26, 1994, with their instructors.

Pictured from left to right are Honor Guard members in 1995: agent Jim Bell, officers Mike Clifton and Jeff Hink, and agent John Wisser. The Honor Guard represents the department at funerals for fallen officers and other formal events.

Officers Maureen Hyde (second from left) and Dan Richey (third from left) pose with "the brass" upon their graduation from the Los Angeles County Sheriff's Academy in 1995. Pictured with the graduates are, from left to right, Los Angeles County sheriff Sherman Block, Chief Mel Nichols, and captains Jeff Cameron and Steve Murdoch. RBPD utilizes several basic academies to provide basic training for its officers depending upon availability. In the past, these have also included Riverside County Sheriff, Orange County Sheriff, Golden West College, and Rio Hondo College.

The motor unit on a training ride to Ojai is seen engaging in positive community-oriented policing. From left to right are officers Bob Sevilla (kneeling) and Jim Booth, Sgt. Bruce Rosin, and officers Phil Garcia, Mike Adye, Tom Krafick, Jim Banach, and Jeff Hink.

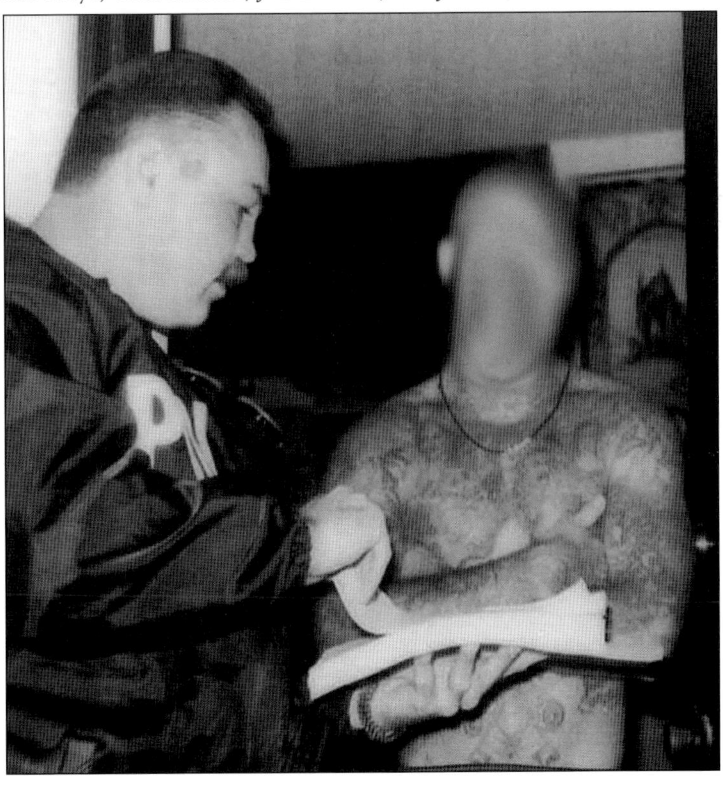

Officer Doug Peters serves gang injunction notification papers to a documented gang member in 1995. Earlier that year, the Redondo Beach Police Department, working in conjunction with the Redondo Beach City Prosecutor's Office, won an injunction prohibiting a street gang from entering a local park that the gang had been terrorizing. The injunction lowered violent crime in and around the park by over 80 percent in one year.

The Volunteers in Policing Program (VIPs) began in 1995 as the department embraced the concept of community-oriented policing. VIPs took responsibility for many routine patrol functions, allowing patrol officers to focus on problem-solving activities. Shown from left to right with a group of children in the early 1990s are VIPs Mike O'Sullivan and Stanley Bender.

The gang injunction effort gained national recognition, which resulted in presidential candidate Bob Dole visiting the park on his presidential campaign tour. Pictured with candidate Dole (center) are, from left to right, Sgt. Phil Keenan, officers Diane Goldstein and Bob Remington, city prosecutor Mike Webb, and captains Jeff Cameron and Steve Murdoch.

Since the early 1970s, the Redondo Beach Police Department and Redondo Beach Police Officers' Association have collaborated on sending "Santa's Sleigh" through the neighborhoods of Redondo Beach every Christmas season. Now joined by the Fire Fighters' Association, "Santa and his Elves," as well as the entire escort, are all employees or volunteers of these departments. These volunteers donate their time over the month of December to take the sleigh down every street in the city, passing out candy canes and receiving Christmas wishes from every good little boy and girl. Pictured here with Santa are officer Maureen Hyde (left) and Community Service Officer (CSO) Sharon Rose.

From left to right, officers Mike Clifton and Jim Banach, agent Rich Sigler, and his K-9 partner Ajax search for a suspected narcotics dealer. (Photograph courtesy of *Daily Breeze*.)

RBPD medal winners are seen at a Los Angeles County Sheriff's "Mud Run" event at Wayside Honor Rancho on September 14, 1997. The Redondo Team took first place among the more than 40 teams that were competing. From left to right are Todd Heywood, Russ Peltz, Bruce Rosin, Mike Adye, and Rich Sigler.

The Pier Unit is depicted above in 1998. From left to right are CSO Sandra Cox, officer Dave Christian, agent Ron Krajcik, officer Bud Johnson, Sgt. John Gordon, and officers Joe Hoffman, Mike Snakenborg, Shawn Freeman, and Phyllis Akers.

From June 1997 until April 1998, the Redondo Beach, Torrance, and Palos Verdes Estates Police Departments ran an undercover storefront operation on Artesia Boulevard. This operation, known as "Bull Market," resulted in the purchase and recovery of $4.3 million in stolen property, which included 212 stolen cars. A total of 96 individuals were arrested with 540 felony counts filed. All transactions were video recorded, which helped in attaining a 100 percent conviction rate. This program earned the City of Redondo Beach the California League of Cities prestigious Helen Putnam Award as best project for 1998.

Operation Bull Market

Located at IVD Enterprises, 2218A Artesia Blvd. IVD in Roman numerals equals 496, the Penal Code section for possession of stolen property.

The suspects

- **96, 78** of whom have been arrested.
- **84** have prior felonies.
- **39 are gang members** or have known gang affiliations.
- **539 felony counts** filed, including armed robbery, carjacking, grand theft, receiving stolen property, auto theft, solicitation of stolen property and perjury.

The police

- **Team involved in raids:** 75 officers from Redondo Beach, Torrance and El Segundo.

The dollars

- **Cost to police:** $181,000.
- **Property recovered:** $4.3 million in stolen goods recovered, including 212 vehicles.

Police agencies involved in the investigation: Redondo Beach, Torrance, El Segundo, Sheriff's Department, state Department of Justice, District Attorney's Office, U.S. Secret Service, U.S. Postal Service, Inglewood, Beverly Hills, Palos Verdes Estates, Hawthorne, TRAP team and L.A. IMPACT.

At the culmination of Operation Bull Market, Gov. Pete Wilson (center) attended the press conference where he proclaimed the program the "most successful sting operation in California history." Shown with the governor are, from left to right, officer Marina Morales, Sgt. John Simmons, officers Rody Contreras and Jim Booth, Lt. John Skipper, and officers Maureen Hyde, Tom Dorsey (Torrance PD), and Kevin McCamy.

The Command Staff congratulates officer Marina Morales (second from left) on the successful conclusion of Operation Bull Market. Seen with Morales are, from left to right, captains Jeff Cameron and Steve Murdoch and Chief Mel Nichols.

From left to right, John Wisser, Mike Adye, Bruce Rosin, Fred Schumaker, and Russ Peltz negotiate an obstacle at the "Mud Run" in the mid-1990s.

Six

A New Millennium, Our Future Begins 2001–Present

Lt. Bruce Rosin coordinated this "End of the Millennium" department photograph, taken New Year's Eve 1999 when the entire department was mandated to work in anticipation of Y2K. To facilitate the photograph, the Torrance Police Department took over patrol duties in Redondo Beach for one hour.

Reserve officer Mike Stark (left) poses with Capt. Steve Murdoch in front of the Reserve Officers Booth at the Redondo Beach Community Safety Fair in October 2001. The Redondo Beach Community Safety Fair is an annual event hosted by the city where residents can view demonstrations, tour the police department, and meet city officials.

Sgt. Phil Keenan examines a silencer-equipped firearm seized during a raid in 2001. Also seized were seven pipe bombs and 60 pounds of explosives.

In tuxedos, from left to right, officers Shawn Freeman, Terry Jones, and Mike Dyberg vie for the attention of the audience during the South Bay Police and Fire Memorial Foundation's annual bachelor auction in 2001, a charity event used to raise funds for the South Bay Police and Fire Memorial Foundation. Officer Freeman met his wife, Michelle, at this event. Officer Jones instigated a bidding war between two hopeful women that earned him the highest auction bid of the evening.

Members of the police department's SWAT team participate in the Los Angeles County Sheriff's Department's annual Special Enforcement Bureau Mud Run in 2001 at the Peter J. Pitchess Honor Rancho in Castaic, California.

In 2001, Gen. Norman Schwarzkopf appeared at the Redondo Beach Performing Arts Center as part of the Distinguished Speaker Series. When Redondo Beach Police Department lieutenant Bruce Rosin, a Vietnam veteran, went backstage after the speech to get an autograph, Schwarzkopf noticed Rosin's Americal Division lapel pin. The general, who had also served in the Americal Division, reached out and took Rosin's hand, and as they shook hands, General Schwarzkopf said to Lieutenant Rosin, "Thank you for serving our country."

School Resource Officers (SRO) Mike Vitalich (left) and Ed Jackson present a recognition award to Adam Sloey, a Redondo Union High School student. This award is based on overall scholastic and athletic ability. The goal of the program is to foster good relations between the general student body and the police department. The SRO program grew out of the department's commitment to community-oriented policing, and the SROs serve as a vital link between the department and school district.

Officer Fernando Mata (left) and Sgt. Mark Klempa utilize the watch commander's command post vehicle to establish incident command at an event in 2002.

After the September 11 terrorist attacks, police departments nationwide began taking a more active role in counterterrorist training. In 2002, Redondo Beach sent a contingent to Northern Ireland, where it studied techniques of dealing with terrorism in a democratic society as practiced by the Police Service of Northern Ireland. Seen here in front of an elaborate paramilitary mural are, from left to right, Redondo Beach city prosecutor Mike Webb, Sgt. Phil Keenan, and Lt. John Skipper.

Volunteers in Policing (VIP) members are pictured above in 2002. From left to right are (front) Capt. Steve Murdoch, Lynne Bowman, Ken McWaid, Heling Craig, Jeni Stimson, Patricia Cutten, Christa Poole, and Chief Robert Lumen; (second row) Lt. Joe Leonardi; Sgt. Bob Remington; VIPs Mark Hoffman, Jim Thompson, Bob McElhaney, Bob Allison, Claude Navarette, and Leon Kahine; and officer Mike Diehr; (third row) VIPs Eric Moberg, Henry Vandenbrink, Milt Sherman, Bob Woodward, John Bullock, Barbara Craig, and Bert Bruning.

The Redondo Beach Police Department's annual Public Safety Fair and Open House is always a big hit with community members. From left to right, officer Ken Greenleaf watches as reserve officers Jack Dickert, Steve Murdoch, and Bill Mona prepare the hot dogs that help keep the public coming back for more each year.

Chief Robert Luman (far right, standing) poses with other members of the RBPD's Investigations Division during its annual holiday party in December 2004.

Officers Maureen Hyde (center, kneeling) and Cory King (second from right) pose with members of the South Bay Gang Task Force (SBGTF) in 2004. Officer Hyde founded the SBGTF in 1998 to improve interagency cooperation and information sharing and to enhance the control of gang-related crime in Redondo Beach and the South Bay. The SBGTF sweep initially had 12 interagency participants; it later had as many as 60.

In 2004, members of the Special Investigations Unit (SIU) solicited the assistance of the California Air National Guard in Point Mugu, California, to obtain surveillance photographs of a residence of a suspected narcotics trafficker. The C-130 aircraft pictured here was used to take the photographs. Posing in front of the aircraft are, from left to right, (kneeling) detectives Mike Vitalich, Rex Fowler (El Segundo PD), and Scot Martin; (standing) detective sergeant Joe Hoffman and detectives Corey King, Jon Naylor, and Shawn Freeman.

As a response to the terrorism threat and in an effort to help provide resources to local law enforcement, several RBPD members and the city prosecutor formed a nonprofit organization—The Foundation for Combating Terrorism and Transnational Crime. The foundation donated equipment, including four explosive-detecting canines, to a variety of local and federal law enforcement agencies and collected bulletproof vests and other safety equipment being discarded by U.S. law enforcement agencies (but still in useable condition) and gave them to developing law enforcement agencies in Iraq and Afghanistan. In this photograph, Sgt. Phil Keenan (left) and Capt. John Skipper (right) pose with two Southern California soldiers in Kabul, Afghanistan, while making a delivery of over 600 bulletproof vests in 2005.

Members of the Redondo Beach Police Department gather with six new RBPD officers (wearing white gloves) to celebrate their graduation from Los Angeles County Sheriff's Department Academy Class No. 341. From left to right are officer Matt Knott, Chief Robert Luman, officer Brian Long, Lt. Tom Eskridge, officer Delvin Delery, Lt. Paul Wrightsman, officer Bob Bassinger, Lt. Jim Acquarelli, Capt. Joe Leonardi, officer Blake Nimmons, Lt. Tom Krafick, officer Jason Sapienm and retired agent and background coordinator Dave Atwater.

The police department and family members celebrate with reserve officer Mike Stark in 2005 after he was awarded the State of California Reserve Police Officer of the Year at the California Reserve Police Officer's Association conference in San Diego, California. Pictured from left to right are Tracy Stark (Mike's wife), Mike Stark, Joan Stark (Mike's mom), and Chief Robert Lumen.

In 2005, Special Investigations Unit detectives initiated an investigation into the use of boats to illegally traffic marijuana across the border. The investigation led to the seizure of a vessel and over 800 pounds of marijuana. With the many bundles of recovered marijuana are, from left to right, detectives Jon Naylor, Corey King, Mike Vitalich, Rex Fowler (ESPD), and Scot Martin, detective sergeant Joe Hoffman, and detective Shawn Freeman.

SWAT entry team members conduct a dangerous mission in 2005. In addition to barricaded suspect missions, the SWAT team annually serves dozens of high-risk search warrants, as depicted here.

In 2005, the RBPD SWAT team went to Camp Pendelton to train members of Joel Peters's marine unit in building entry prior to their deployment to Iraq. Joel Peters is the son of RBPD officer Doug Peters, standing on far left. SWAT members in the dark uniforms at the left are, from left to right, (kneeling) officer Dan Richey and Sgt. Todd Heywood; (standing) officers Delvin Delery and Mike Martinez.

This family affair depicts reserve officer Mike Stark (center) with brothers Lt. Tom Stark (left) and officer Tim Stark, both members of the Torrance Police Department. Mike holds the recognition he received from the City of Redondo Beach for being awarded the 2005 State of California Reserve Police Officer of the Year.

Police Department Records Unit employees provide invaluable assistance during the Amgen Tour of California in 2006. Pictured are, from left to right, cadet Brenda Mireles, PSS Tonya Pracht, Lead PSS Charley Clark, and PSS Mechell Divinity. Redondo Beach served as the final leg of the inaugural race that began in Northern California and attracted hundreds of thousands of spectators along the route. The Amgen Tour is one of the largest cycling events in America.

Officer Lori Shimkus watches over the hundreds of bicyclists who competed in the 2006 Amgen Tour of California.

Officer Ken Greenleaf (left) and officer Kevin McCamy introduce the newest members of the Redondo Beach Police Department, canines Valor (left) and Kona, at a city council meeting in 2006.

Members of the Investigations Division pose with contraband seized in a raid in 2006. From left to right are detectives Mark Sturgeon, Lori Shimkus, Denise Brenner, Leonard Jordan, Fabian Saucedo, Mike Strosnider, Rick Kochheim, Ed Jackson, and Alan Beck and Sgt. Pete Grimm.

Retired sergeant Mike Worford, Lt. Wayne Windman, and officer John Erwin are seen at the American Cancer Society's Relay for Life in 2006. Police department personnel have participated yearly in this event since 2000, and the tri-tip dinner prepared by these officers is always in high demand.

Reserve officer Royce Branch has been a member of the department for 36 years. He is also an automobile racing enthusiast. Royce built this car and used it to represent the department at a variety of community functions and events. The car currently holds the speed record for the fastest "chartered" police car in the United States, having traveled at 189 miles per hour at the Bonneville Salt Flats in 2008. He hopes to exceed 200 miles per hour in the near future.

Officers shared in the carrying of the torch in 2006 during the annual Law Enforcement Special Olympics Torch Run benefitting the Special Olympics. Participating are, from left to right, Sgt. John Wisser, officer Ellen Tumbocon, reserve officer Mike Stark, officers Scott Martin and Michael Strosnider, and Lt. Joe Hoffman.

Officer Kevin McCamy and canine Kirby look for hidden narcotics during a multiagency interdiction deployment at a border-crossing checkpoint in 2007.

The police department has routinely dedicated additional personnel to patrol the Redondo Beach Pier and beach each summer in response to the increased number of visitors and tourists. In this 2007 photograph are, from left to right, reserve officer Barry Brennan, Sgt. Phil Keenan, officer Marina Morales, and reserve officer Mike Stark.

In 2005, officer Doug Peters's son Joel, a U.S. Marine, was deployed to Iraq. During his deployment, Joel presented the Redondo Beach Police Department with a U.S. flag that was flown over his air base. The flag was placed in a presentation frame and is on display in the police department. Pictured from left to right are Chief Joe Leonardi, Capt. Tom Krafick, officer Doug Peters, Sgt. Rick Kochheim, Municipal Service Office (MSO) supervisor Pattie Ziello, Lt. Paul Wrightsman, Sgt. Mike Adye, Lt. Todd Heywood, and executive assistant Renate Bryant.

Officer Ryan Crespin (right) provides instruction in the proper use of the Redondo Beach Police Department's Segway human transporter to officer Robert Carlborg at the Redondo Beach Pier. The police department was the first South Bay agency to purchase the Segway for law enforcement use. Officers used the transporter to patrol the pier and the South Bay Galleria.

The SWAT team trains monthly to insure its proficiency in the latest tactics and deployment strategies. In this photograph, SWAT members are practicing waterborne tactics with the Harbor Patrol.

Crime Scene Investigation officer Maureen Hyde analyzes a piece of evidence for fingerprints in the police department's crime lab in 2008.

Emergency Services dispatcher Nicole Bavis displays her skill at dispatching one of the tens of thousands of emergency 911 calls received annually by the police department's Communications Unit.

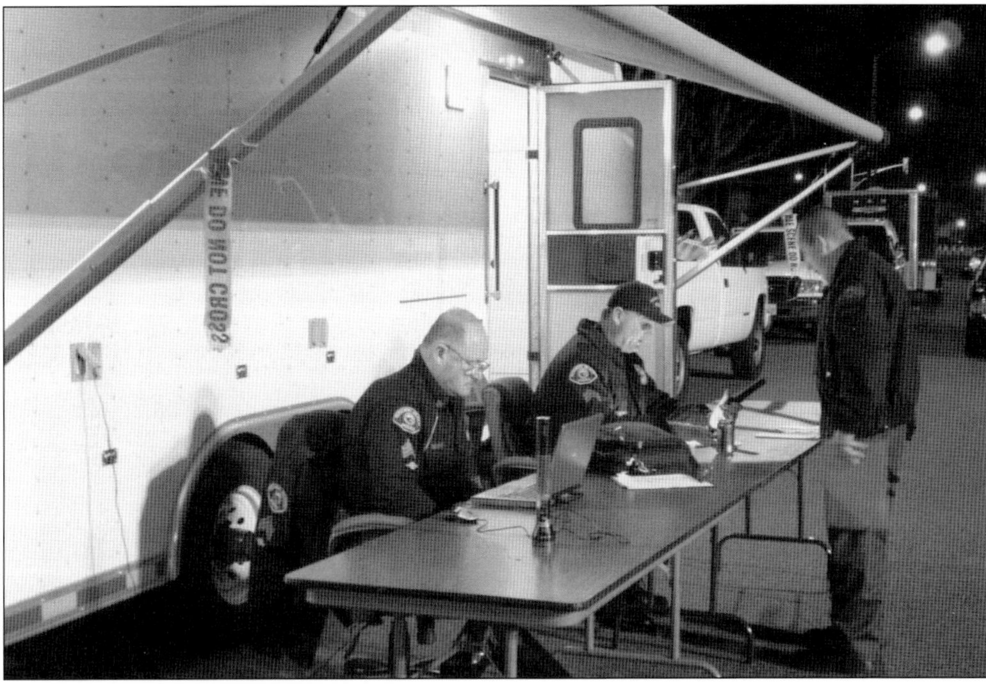

Sergeants Mike Adye (left) and John McIntosh with cadet Richard Saldana review arrest reports outside of the Redondo Beach Police Department's command post trailer at one of the Driving Under the Influence traffic checkpoints in 2008.

After the attacks of September 11, 2001, the Redondo Beach Police Department became the first South Bay agency to assign a detective to the FBI's Joint Terrorism Task Force (JTTF). After being assigned, detective Jeff Hink was deployed to Guantanamo Bay, Cuba (GTMO), in 2002, for 45 days, where he partnered with the military to interview enemy combatants. In this 2008 photograph, detective Chris Sosenko is seen near the main gates at GTMO. Detective Sosenko was the second Redondo Beach officer to be so deployed.

Members of the police department's SWAT team pose with the South Bay Armored Response Vehicle (ARV) during a training event in 2008. The ARV was purchased in 2007 after the police department obtained federal homeland security funding. The ARV is shared with all of the Area G South Bay cities.

Formal uniform inspections have long been a part of the Redondo Beach Police Department's culture. In this photograph, from left to right, officers Don Martinez, Steve Sabosky, Marina Morales, Maureen Hyde, and Cliff Dean arrive for one of the inspections. Not visible in this photograph are officer Martinez's pink fuzzy bunny rabbit slippers.

At the 2009 Annual Redondo Beach K-9 Trials, Dak negotiates an obstacle while his partner, officer Corey King, looks on. The trials raise money for the department's K-9 program. The Redondo Beach Police Department has sponsored this multiagency event for over 23 years.

LA IMPACT detective Fernando Mata (center) poses with other team members, detective Mike Snakenborg (far left), and the narcotics seized during a high-profile investigation. The Los Angeles Inter-Agency Metropolitan Police Apprehension Crime Task Force (LA IMPACT) was created in the early 1990s to address the dramatic increase in major narcotics trafficking and is comprised of police officers from throughout Los Angeles County.

Detective Fernando Mata poses with a large amount of U.S. currency while he was assigned to LA IMPACT. The money was seized as a result of a major narcotics investigation. The police department began its participation in LA IMPACT after its inception in the early 1990s.

Reserve officers Patricia Boras and Clint Dean give hands-on, all-terrain vehicle training to a future police department recruit in 2009 during the National Night Out event at the Redondo Beach Target store parking lot. The police department has strongly supported the National Night Out event in Redondo Beach each year to promote Neighborhood Watch and the police-community partnership.

The Crisis Negotiations Vehicle is on display at the 2009 Community Safety Fair. The Crisis Negotiations Team (CNT) trains quarterly with SWAT and other South Bay police agencies to insure interagency cooperation and readiness. The CNT also works closely with SWAT and other units to establish communications and defuse the danger with persons who barricade themselves or refuse to cooperate with the police. Pictured are CNT members Sgt. Dave Taneman (left) and reserve officer Mike Stark.

Volunteers in Policing (VIP) member Larry Brehm (center) assists the SWAT team and the Crisis Negotiation Team during the Redondo Beach Police Department's 2009 Community Safety Fair demonstration. From left to right are SWAT team officers Philip Ho and Delvin Delery, VIP Brehm, SWAT team lieutenant Todd Heywood, CNT member reserve officer Mike Stark, and SWAT team member detective Mike Martinez.

The South Bay Platoon was established in the 1990s as a result of the civil unrest that occurred after the trial verdicts for the Los Angeles Police Department officers who were accused of beating Rodney King. The purpose of the platoon was to standardize the South Bay law enforcement agency response to incidents involving civil unrest and to improve and enhance riot training for officers. Redondo Beach Police Department members of the South Bay Platoon stand next to the South Bay Area G Command Vehicle during a deployment for a demonstration in 2009. Pictured are, from left to right, (first row) officers Blake Nimmons and Jim Booth, Lt. Jim Acquarelli, and officers Denise Brenner and Alan Beck; (second row) officers Dan Smith, Steve Sprengel, and Matt Knott, sergeants Jon Naylor and David Taneman, officer Chris Sabosky, and Sgt. John McIntosh.

Angela Prestia proudly pins the badge on her newly promoted husband, Sgt. Chuck Prestia, in January 2009. Both Angela and Chuck were former cadets at the department.

Chief Joe Leonardi conducts the swearing-in ceremony for MSO Pedro Malo in 2008. The MSOs are responsible for animal control and parking enforcement duties within the city.

Redondo Beach Police Department members participate in the American Cancer Society's Relay for Life on Team Lifesavers in 2009. From left to right are retired sergeant Mike Worford Sr., crime analyst Dawn Switzer, officer John Bruce, retired sergeant and cocaptain Mark Klempa, cocaptain Rick Hefner, and officer Maureen Hyde.

Members of the Redondo Beach Police Department attend an awards ceremony in 2010. Pictured are, from left to right, captains Tom Krafick and Jeff Hink, officer Corey King, Lt. Jim Acquarelli, officers Cliff Dean and Bud Johnson, personnel and training manager Judy Durham, officer Bill Turner Sr., crime analyst Dawn Switzer, reserve officer Royce Branch, Lead PSS Charley Clark, CSO II Frank Watt, domestic violence coordinator Erica Gonzalez, and Chief Joe Leonardi. Not pictured are reserve officer Paul Decker, Rabbi Leon Kahane, officers Walt Sawall and Jeff Sumners, K-9 officer Ken Greenleaf, and clerical assistant Joseph Ott, who were also recognized at the ceremony.

Members of the Redondo Beach Police Department's Baker to Vegas "Surf 2 Sand" running team participate in a spaghetti dinner fundraising event in 2010. From left to right are officers Catherine Saade and Alan Beck, retired agent Rich Sigler, officer Denise Brenner, Capt. Jeff Hink, and officers Ian Miesen and Ellen Tumbocon. The Challenge Cup–Baker to Vegas Relay is a 120-mile relay race in which police departments from all over the world traverse a course from Baker through the Southern California and Nevada deserts and end in Las Vegas.

Crime Scene Investigations officers Blake Nimmons (right) and Walter Sawall search a trash dumpster looking for evidence in 2010.

Officer Mike Dyberg (left) and Sgt. Paul Burch demonstrate the benefits of their assignment in 2010.

Members of the RBPD's Traffic Unit are seen at the Redondo Beach Pier in 2010. From left to right are traffic investigator Jeff Mendence, officer Scott Martin, Sgt. Paul Burch, and officers Mike Dyberg and Matt Knott. In 2010, the department was notified that it had placed third in the 2009 California Law Enforcement Challenge. This award was presented to RBPD due to the traffic enforcement efforts of patrol and traffic and the department's "outstanding efforts in traffic safety."

Officers Edward Jackson (left) and Ryan Crespin sharpen their defensive tactics skills at a 2010 police department training day.

Retired captain Jeff Cameron was also a captain in the U.S. Naval Reserve, assigned to the Naval Criminal Investigative Service. Captain Cameron has been deployed to the Persian Gulf and other locations worldwide several times in support of the global war on terror.

Officer Brian Weiss, a member of the U.S. Marine Corps Reserve, was called to active duty in 2009 and served a tour of duty in Afghanistan. Officer Weiss returned home safely in June 2010.

Chiefs of Police

1882–1920

S. P. Rogers, 1882–1883
George Foyer, 1883–1894
Silas Blanchard, 1894–1896
E. P. Maxey, 1896–1900
L. J. Woolley, 1900–1902
E. P. Maxey, 1902–1904
J. K. Smith, 1904–1906
E. P. Maxey, 1906–1907
Lee Stanchfield, 1907–1912
Al Lambert, 1912
John Perdue, 1912–1914
Eli Moiser, 1914–1920

1920–Present

The following men are pictured from left to right, top to bottom:
John V. Henry, 1920–1928
Harry M. Petersen, 1928–1947
Lowell Hopkins, 1947–1956
Curt Richardson, 1956–1963
Robert Mutch (interim), 1963–1964
William A. Bechtel, 1964–1967
Harvey Lord (interim), 1967–1968
Louis J. Sunyich, 1968–1975
Frank V. Meehan, 1975–1983
Allen D. Woods (interim), 1983–1984
Roger M. Moulton, 1984–1993
Roger Bass (interim), 1993
Melvin E. Nichols, 1993–2001
Stephen R. Murdoch (interim), 2001–2002
Robert M. Luman, 2002–2006
W. Joseph Leonardi, 2006–present